"Movements aren't sustained by
preaching and writing alone . . . "

" . . . but by the music and art that communicate the vision of the movement."

— Steve Murrell (President, Every Nation)

EVERY NATION
MUSIC

WORSHIP WRITERS WORKBOOK

A WORKBOOK
FOR CHRISTIAN SONGWRITERS
WANTING TO WRITE SONGS
WITH GOOD THEOLOGY,
GOSPEL MISSION,
AND GLOBAL DIVERSITY.

TABLE OF CONTENTS

PREFACE

As the president and cofounder of a global movement of churches, I think a lot about the future of our young movement. While I have personally spent more time shaping sermons than setlists, as I have gotten older, I've come to see the important role that music plays in shaping us.

Gordon Fee once wrote, "Show me a church's music, and I'll show you their theology." In other words, the songs we sing may shape more of our theology than the words a preacher shares. As songwriters, I hope you recognize the tremendous opportunity you have to impact congregations—not just of today, but of generations to come. Years ago, when John Newton—reflecting on the brokenness and redemption in his life—penned "Amazing Grace," I doubt he could have ever imagined the reach and significance of his simple song.

As you develop the craft of songwriting, I pray that you think about the people who, one day, will be singing your songs. I hope that you remember how songs have a remarkable ability to remind us of who God is, who we are, and what we are called to do. As you write, remember Gordon Fee's words. Whether you're shaping words into lyrics or notes into a melody, you have the power to impact generations for the glory of God.

Steve Murrell
President, Every Nation

WHY THIS BOOK?

Worship music is an integral part of how we engage God. So it's important that our music not only be creatively inspiring but also anchored in scripture and biblical community. For the last several years, we have worked to cultivate a global community of songwriters to serve the local church by writing songs that are technically sound and theologically accurate.

We believe that anyone can make a significant musical contribution to how God is worshipped in the nations of the world. Which brings us to you—if you're reading this book, you have an interest in songwriting and we want to help you.

As you work through this book, here are a few questions to ask yourself:

1. *What is it about writing songs privately and/or in community that you enjoy?*

2. *How often do you write songs that help people connect with God in a deeper way?*

3. *How has songwriting affected your ability to connect with God?*

4. *If someone says "worship" does songwriting naturally come to mind?*

5. *How do you view songwriting in relationship to your current ministry and future legacy?*

As you meditate on these questions, you will hopefully form a clearer picture of how God has uniquely fashioned you. Keep in mind that your identity is found in your relationship with God and his plans for you are good.

"For we are his workmanship, created in Christ Jesus for good works, which God prepared beforehand, that we should walk in them."
— Ephesians 2:10

This book is designed to cultivate your skill, creativity, and engagement as a songwriter. Each chapter concludes with a time of reflection and at least thirty minutes of songwriting. Challenge yourself to be consistent.

Throughout the book, we've provided annotations as additional information on the chapter subject.

On page 119, we've provided blank journal space for you to write up to fifty songs.

Songwriting is deeply embedded in the story of God's people and has helped to preserve our spiritual heritage and propagate the gospel message.

THE CHURCH

Objective: At the conclusion of this section, you will have an understanding of diverse expressions of worship and the role of songwriting throughout church history. This will help to provide motivation and context for the importance of songwriting.

SECTION

"For you, O LORD, have made me
glad by your work; at the works
of your hands I sing for joy."

– Psalm 92:4

CHAPTER 1:
THE STORY
OF WORSHIP
SONGWRITING

For thousands of years, music has played an important role in communicating God's instruction, mission, and desire for community. The first two songs in the Bible were written by Moses: the first being the creation story of Genesis chapters 1 and 2, and the second with his sister, Miriam, found in Exodus 15:1–21. Since the time of God's deliverance of the Israelites, the people of God have used songwriting as a tool to preserve and celebrate God's redemptive work. In this chapter, we'll take a snapshot of various periods in church history that have shaped the way we understand the relationship between music and worship today.

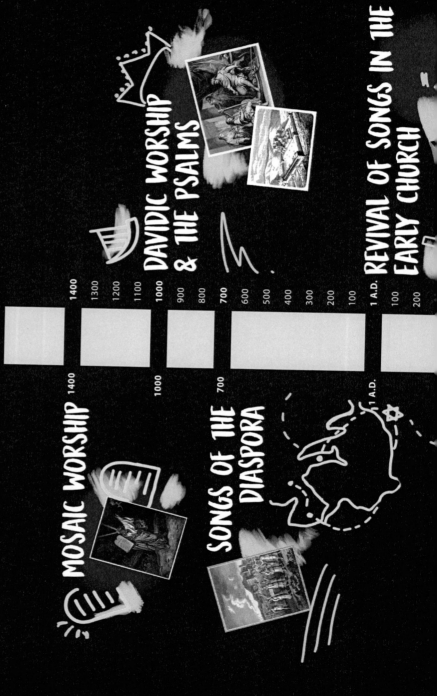

Mosaic Worship (1400 B.C.)

Moses and Miriam's song in Exodus 15 was in response to the Israelites' deliverance from Egyptian captivity. Although this act of worship was sincere and truthful, it wasn't until God gave Moses the Ten Commandments and sacrificial system that worship relationship would be formally defined. This formal definition of worship was important because a common feature of ancient Near-Eastern culture was polytheism (i.e. the belief in or worship of more than one god). Without God giving strict guidelines for this new worship relationship, the Israelite people would have tried to mix pagan practices with worship of Yahweh.

This new worship system was led by Moses, his older brother Aaron, and the Levites. True worship could only be administered by this Levitical community of priests which would have limited worship songwriting to God's appointed ministry leaders. Music was not a major component of worship during this time. However, the law of Moses and Levitical priesthood were not to be instituted indefinitely.

God used this strict worship pattern to shape the heart response of his people to continue in covenant faithfulness and this would eventually give way to a more musical and spontaneous worship expression.

Davidic Worship & the Psalms (1000 B.C.)

With the reign of King David came a big shift in worship practice because God finally found "a man after [his] own heart" (1 Sam 13:14). David was careful to maintain observance of the Mosaic worship system but understood that more than rituals and sacrifices, God desired heartfelt devotion and obedience. This ushered in a significant time of spiritual revival in Israel where the Spirit of God was manifested in powerful ways.

"Davidic worship was not based on ritual or ceremony but was a spontaneous response to the moving of God's Spirit. For this reason it could not be passed to succeeding generations of Israelites, as was the Mosaic sacrificial system."
— worshiplibrary.com

Although the spontaneous nature of Davidic worship could not be replicated, David's heart passion was transmitted through his songwriting. These songs would continue to shape the liturgical practices of God's people for generations. For over 3,000 years the book of the Bible known as Psalms has served as a means of inspiration, praise, worship, and communion with God for the Judeo-Christian community. The word "psalmos" in the Greek is actually translated into Hebrew as "song."

The Psalms point us to the idea that God is interested and involved in every aspect of our lives. They serve as a model of the freedom we have to intimately express ourselves to God through our worship relationship.

The poetic writings of King David and his fellow psalmists cover a robust spectrum of thoughts, emotions, and "God interactions" as illustrated in the verses below.

"Be gracious to me, O LORD, for I am languishing; heal me, O LORD, for my bones are troubled. My soul also is greatly troubled. But you, O LORD—how long?"
– Psalm 6:2–3

"I pour out my complaint before him; I tell my trouble before him."
– Psalm 142:2

"Search me, O God, and know my heart! Try me and know my thoughts!"
– Psalm 139:23

"For you, O LORD, have made me glad by your work; at the works of your hands I sing for joy."
– Psalm 92:4

Songs of the Diaspora (722 B.C.–1 B.C.)

Following the reign of King David, worship continued through the leadership of his son Solomon. Solomon was recognized as a man of great wisdom and insight and is most noted for his prolific writing. He is credited with writing over 1,000 songs including the most notable Song of Solomon. Under his leadership, the temple was built as the primary gathering place for the Israelites to encounter God through sacrificial worship. Solomon's temple represented a place of protection and preservation of Israelite worship practices. It symbolized God in the midst of his people.

After Solomon's reign, Israel was split into two nations which would eventually lead to several foreign invasions, the destruction of the temple, and the scattering of the Jewish people. In order to preserve the cultural and religious identity of Jews in exile, God raised up prophets to call God's people to covenant faithfulness. Many times these prophets used songs as a means to warn God's people of judgement or remind them of his promises. The lamentations of Ezekiel, as well as Isaiah's outcries for Israel's protection, are examples of song in prophetic ministry.

The last song of the Old Testament is recorded in Habakkuk 3:2

"LORD, I have heard the report about You and I fear. O LORD, revive Your work in the midst of the years, In the midst of the years make it known; In wrath remember mercy."

19

"How you have perished, O inhabited one,
From the seas, O renowned city,
Which was mighty on the sea,

She and her inhabitants,
Who imposed her terror
On all her inhabitants!

Now the coastlands will tremble
On the day of your fall;
Yes, the coastlands which are by the sea
Will be terrified at your passing."
— Ezekiel 26:17—18

"In that day this song will be
sung in the land of Judah:
'We have a strong city;

He sets up walls and ramparts for security.
Open the gates, that the
righteous nation may enter.
The one that remains faithful.
The steadfast of mind You will
keep in perfect peace,
Because he trusts in You.

Trust in the Lord forever.
For in God the Lord, we have
an everlasting Rock.
For He has brought low those who
dwell on high, the unassailable city;
He lays it low, He lays it low to the
ground, He casts it to the dust.

The foot will trample it.
The feet of the afflicted, the
steps of the helpless."

– Isaiah 26:1–6

Revival of Songs in the Early Church (1 A.D.–400's)

The cultural assimilation of the Jewish people into foreign nations significantly affected their sense of tradition and worship practices. This continued to varying degrees throughout the Jewish diaspora until the time of Jesus. Jewish synagogues eventually became cultural/religious centers of prayer, praise, and instruction of the Torah.

Jesus and his disciples participated in these Jewish traditions; however, Jesus challenged the status quo of synagogue worship by his divine authority as Immanuel, "God with us." He overturned the religious system that only allowed the righteous to worship by calling for repentance and exercising his power to forgive sins.

After the death and resurrection of Jesus, the apostles were commissioned to bring the gospel to all nations. Embedded in this idea was the expansion of true worship from a specific people and place into the daily lives of Christ followers.

Empowered by the Holy Spirit, the early church experienced revival in congregational singing and promoted spontaneous worship. The following scriptures give us insight into this new reality:

"About midnight Paul and Silas were praying and singing hymns to God, and the prisoners were listening to them, and suddenly there was a great earthquake, so that the foundations of the prison were shaken. And immediately all the doors were opened, and everyone's bonds were unfastened."
— Acts 16:25–26

In the above passage, Paul and Silas prayed and sang songs as a declaration of God's goodness in spite of harsh circumstances. Without a temple or Torah, they transformed a prison into a place of worship. The impact of their prayers and singing was not only experienced personally but also instrumental in ministering to those around them.

"Let the word of Christ dwell in you richly, teaching and admonishing one another in all wisdom, singing psalms and hymns and spiritual songs, with thankfulness in your hearts to God."
— Colossians 3:16

In Paul's letter to the church in Colossae, he admonishes them to sing as a means to cultivate the word of Christ in their hearts. Singing was vital in stirring their devotion and affection for this cosmic Christ who holds all things together by the word of his power (Colossians 1:17).

"And they were singing a new song before the throne and before the four living creatures and before the elders. No one could learn that song except the 144,000 who had been redeemed from the earth."
— Revelation 14:3

This final passage highlights the song of redemption sung throughout eternity celebrating God's victory over sin through the spotless Lamb of God—Jesus. Congregational singing continued to evolve throughout the earliest period of Christianity. Specifically, Paul and Barnabas' ministry to the Gentiles began to influence Christian worship by embracing non-Jewish worship practices. The spread of the gospel throughout the world created many tensions between Jewish and Gentile worship traditions. This would be the beginning of many discussions and changes in worship practices for the Christian community.

Music in the Middle Ages (400's–1500's)

Following the death of the apostles, the influence of Christianity continued to flourish despite severe social and political opposition. Roman persecution led to a diaspora as Christians sought refuge in outlying regions. The farther away Christianity moved from the Jewish center of Jerusalem, the less their worship reflected early Jewish tradition. In order to keep the unity of the faith and a firm understanding of the teaching of the apostles, several councils met together to discuss and decide on major doctrinal issues. But they couldn't decide on everything—issues related to music still remained a subject of debate.

Many of the early church fathers had a love/hate relationship with music and at various times in history allowed or banned this kind of creative expression. In the late second century, severe restrictions were placed on worship music for the following reasons:

- Music was related to superstitious and sensual pagan worship.

- Music was suspect for moral reasons.

- It was seen to favor the flesh over the Spirit.

"John Chrysostom condemned musical instruments, along with dancing and obscene songs, as being the 'Devil's garbage'. "

— Richard Viladesau Jr.,Theology and the Arts, pg. 15

"And safer to me seems what I remember was often told me concerning Athanasius, bishop of Alexandria, who required the reader of the psalm to perform it with so little inflection of voice that it was closer to speaking than to singing."
— Saint Augustine

*Below is a list of **key features of Orthodox and Coptic church traditions** which have played a role in the preservation and development of church music and congregational singing:*

- *The Greek Orthodox church is credited with over 60,000 hymns written for use during their services.*

- *The liturgy of most Orthodox churches is sung from beginning to end.*

- *There is historical evidence to suggest that Coptic and Ethiopian churches have, at present, music and worship customs that have survived since the earliest periods of Christianity.*

- *The liturgical tradition of Ethiopian churches requires that priests spend up to twenty years or more educating themselves in theology, music, art, poetry, and dance as a rite of passage into ministry.*

In all fairness, St. Augustine was not opposed to music, but he, like many others before him, wrestled with the idea of music overpowering the biblical message. His view was one shared by many of the early church fathers until the Chalcedonian schism in AD 451 when the Orthodox and Coptic churches of Mediterranean countries, Eastern Europe, and Northern Africa separated from the Roman Catholic tradition.

If not for the strong interdependence of music and liturgy, the Orthodox and Coptic churches may not have survived to today. In these Christian communities, worship chant and singing were inseparable from the liturgy. For centuries, these churches have preserved their rich Christian heritage by gathering to rehearse biblical truths and the history of faith through music.

It wouldn't be until the papal reign of St. Gregory the Great (AD 590) that the Roman Catholic church would mirror this acceptance of music into liturgy. St. Gregory is credited with significant reforms to Roman liturgy which inspired "Gregorian" chant. This shift in worship practice had a domino effect on both music and liturgy in the Western church. Over time, chanted songs without musical accompaniment reserved for clergy would eventually give way to instruments and more accessible congregational singing.

Reformation Hymns (1500's–1600's)

In the 16th century, Martin Luther's translations of scripture made the biblical text more readily available to the average person. This had a significant impact on the relationship between music and church liturgy. Martin Luther's leadership, as well as other influential ministers during the Protestant reformation, set into motion the common practice of congregational singing.

"It is music alone, according to God's word, that should rightfully be prized as the queen and ruler over every stirring of the human heart . . . What can be more powerful than music to raise the spirits of the sad, to frighten the happy, to make the despondent valiant, to calm those who are enraged, to reconcile those filled with hatred . . . ?"
— Martin Luther

A List of Reformer Hymns:

"A Mighty Fortress Is Our God"
Based on Psalm 46, Martin Luther wrote this impactful "Battle Hymn of the Reformation" in 1529.

"All Glory Be to God on High"
A Roman Catholic monk turned Lutheran teacher, Nikolaus Decius published this hymn in 1525.

"Lord, Thee I Love with All My Heart"
A student of Philipp Melanchthon, Martin Schalling wrote this hymn around 1567.

"Savior of the Nations, Come"
Bishop Ambrose of Milan penned this Latin hymn in the 4th century. Martin Luther prepared a German translation in 1524.

"Once He Came in Blessing"
Johann Roh, a pastor in Bohemia, published this hymn and others in 1544.

This newfound accessibility of scripture provided the opportunity for people to more actively engage in worship. This inspired many of the church reformers to write songs of personal devotion, the power of the gospel, and the work of Christ in the Church.

Revival Songs and the Great Awakenings (1700's–1800's)

The Protestant reformation in Germany sparked a new evolution in worship music and congregational singing around the world. During the 17th and 18th centuries, a group of missionaries and church leaders began to move away from the formal classical chorale sound of the Reformation into more musically diverse songs of personal devotion.

During this time, hymn writers became more sensitive to exploring the experience of biblical truth in the life of the individual. Isaac Watts, writer of some 750 hymns, was instrumental in the development of this style of hymnody. He recognized the need to transition the complex scholastic music of the Reformation to a more vibrant and heartfelt expression of worship.

Contemporaries of Watts, the Wesleys (brothers John and Charles) were also famously noted as the pioneers of "invitation songs," which were evangelistic in nature and called for people to respond to God as an act of their free will. An example of an invitation song is "Come, Sinners, to the Gospel Feast":

"Come, sinners, to the gospel feast,
let every soul be Jesus' guest.
Ye need not one be left behind,
for God hath bid all humankind."
– Charles Wesley

This represented a major shift in congregational singing as songs were not only a medium for the biblical narrative, but also a tool to draw people into relationship with God. Congregational music further evolved as Christian revivals spread throughout Europe, Africa, and the eastern states of America. The spontaneous songs of revivalist "camp meetings" (i.e. outdoor evangelistic gatherings) would have an even greater impact on church liturgy.

These meetings produced a new style of music more accessible to the illiterate population. Many of these new songs set Christian lyrics to popular music which consisted of simple harmonies, memorable melodies, and call/response format.

Contemporary Worship Songs (1900's–Present)

Through the 20th century, worship music has become more central to the global church experience and continues to evolve in style and genre. Today we see the rise of popular styles such as the new hymn (or praise choruses), contemporary christian music (CCM), and black gospel.

THE NEW HYMN

A few notable songs of this era are:

"Take My Hand Precious Lord"
(Thomas A. Dorsey)

"Because He Lives"
(The Gaithers)

"He Touched Me"
(The Gaithers)

"Seek Ye First"
(Karen Ratheby)

As the influence of the church on popular culture expanded during the 20th century, congregational songs became more informal. The classically influenced hymns slowly began to morph into the melodically catchy and simple congregational songs.

These songs still maintained some of the traditional features of the old hymn style but were married with the more memorable "camp meeting" sound. Traveling choirs and bands such as The Fisk Jubilee Singers and The Gaithers became more prevalent during this time spreading this new hymn style throughout various cultures particularly in the United States.

GOSPEL

Northern African countries have a rich tradition of education, storytelling, and community celebration through music. Long before the influence of Western colonization in Africa, these communities flourished with Christian liturgy.

The Colonial Period of the 17th and 18th centuries saw the rise of the African slave trade into Western culture. Music served as a means for slaves to preserve their cultural identity and cryptically communicate with one another about their struggles and hope for freedom. In the United States, this type of musical expression gave birth to the "negro spiritual" and later was synthesized with the western hymn style into what is commonly known as gospel music. Thomas Dorsey, known as the "father of gospel music," composed over 400 songs that blended together spirituals, country, blues, and jazz styles of black American culture. During the early 20th century, the birth of American Pentecostalism helped to spread gospel music throughout church culture in the United States.

Black gospel songs have continued to expand into the mainstream of music culture through innovators such as Kenneth Morris, James Cleveland, Andrae Crouch, The Hawkins Family, The Winans Family, and Kirk Franklin. Through countless changes in culture and style, gospel music's message of spiritual deliverance, hope, and freedom continues to influence Christian music globally.

CCM & PRAISE AND WORSHIP

American Pentecostalism gave birth to the Charismatic Movement of the 1960's and the Jesus Movement of the 1970's. "Jesus Rock" was a revolutionary anti-establishment style of music that grew in popularity parallel with the rise of the secular rock industry. Largely serving as a tool for Christian evangelism, it eventually developed into its own identifiable industry in the 70's and 80's.

Today, this music continues to adapt to the sound of pop culture. Innovators in this genre include Amy Grant, Larry Norman ("Father of Christian Rock Music"), Steven Curtis Chapman, Michael W. Smith, Twila Paris, and Rich Mullins. During the late 80's and early 90's, the subgenre of "praise and worship" began to take shape as churches saw the need for a contemporary way to reimagine biblical themes. Vineyard, Hillsong, and the Passion movement (spearheaded by Chris Tomlin) have become globally recognized as pioneers of the "praise and worship" subgenre.

Shifts in church culture continue to affect worship music through the growing "worship underground." House churches, camp style gatherings, and new grassroots ministries have made a return to folk style hymnody. These songs are characterized by their contemplative, evocative lyrics and electro-acoustic sound. United Pursuit, House Fires, and The Rend Collective are notable "underground" worship artists.

CHAPTER 1 SUMMARY

SONGWRITING IS DEEPLY EMBEDDED IN THE STORY OF GOD'S PEOPLE AND HAS HELPED TO PRESERVE OUR SPIRITUAL HERITAGE AND PROPAGATE THE GOSPEL MESSAGE.

GOD MADE A COVENANT WITH THE ISRAELITES AND DEFINED THE PARAMETERS FOR WORSHIP. SONGWRITING WAS USED AS A TOOL TO PRESERVE AND CELEBRATE GOD'S REDEMPTIVE WORK.

THE PEOPLE OF ISRAEL EXPERIENCED WORSHIP REVIVAL DURING THE REIGN OF KING DAVID WHICH PRODUCED MANY OF THE PSALMS.

MUSIC AND CONGREGATIONAL SINGING DURING THE FIRST SEVERAL CENTURIES OF CHRISTIANITY WAS COMMONLY PRACTICED BUT HIGHLY SCRUTINIZED.

THROUGHOUT HISTORY, SHIFTS IN CHRISTIAN LITURGY HAVE RESULTED IN MORE DIVERSE AND CONGREGATIONAL WORSHIP SONGS.

CHAPTER 1 REFLECTION

How has this historical snapshot impacted your perspective
on songwriting in the Christian community?
How do you see yourself in relation to this story?

CHAPTER 1
WRITING PROMPT

Go to the writing journal section of this book on page 119. Spend at least thirty minutes listening to the hymns referenced in this section and then write a song with those hymns in mind.

"A Mighty Fortress Is Our God"
Based on Psalm 46, Martin Luther wrote this impactful "Battle Hymn of the Reformation" in 1529.

"All Glory Be to God on High"
A Roman Catholic monk turned Lutheran teacher, Nikolaus Decius published this hymn in 1525.

"Lord, Thee I Love with All My Heart"
A student of Philipp Melanchthon, Martin Schalling wrote this hymn around 1567.

"Savior of the Nations, Come"
Bishop Ambrose of Milan penned this Latin hymn in the 4th century. Martin Luther prepared a German translation in 1524.

"Once He Came in Blessing"
Johann Roh, a pastor in Bohemia, published this hymn and others in 1544.

"Take My Hand Precious Lord"
(Thomas A. Dorsey)

"Because He Lives"
(The Gaithers)

"He Touched Me"
(The Gaithers)

"Seek Ye First"
(Karen Ratheby)

The impact of these churches
is survived not only by sermons
and services but by songs.

CHAPTER 2: WHY WE NEED TO WRITE

Based upon the Christian Copyright Licensing International (CCLI) database there are more than 100,000 popular worship songs currently in circulation. You may be thinking, "If the church has plenty of songs to choose from, why is it important for me to contribute?" As we discussed in the previous chapter, an important component of thriving Christian community is the creation of music and art that tells of the story of God's interaction with his people. Every person has something valuable to contribute to the narrative of the advancement of God's kingdom. It's important that you place yourself and your local church within that narrative to draw inspiration for creativity to tell the gospel story.

A Vehicle of Worship

*"Nkosi sikelel' iAfrika
(Lord, bless Africa)*

*Maluphakanyis'
uphondo lwayo (May
her horn rise high up)*

*Yiva imithandazo yethu
(Hear Thou our prayers)*

*Nkosi sikelela, Thina
lusapho lwayo
(And bless us)*

*Yehla Moya, Yehla Moya,
(Descend, O Spirit)*

*Yehla Moya Oyingcwele
(Descend, O Holy Spirit)"*

"Nkosi Sikelel' iAfrika" is unofficially recognized as the national Anthem of South Africa. Originally written by Enoch Sontonga, a methodist minister in 1897, this African hymn represented the outcry of suffering South African people during the apartheid. This song circulated through South African churches for thirty years before finally being published in 1927. Today it has become the national anthem of Zambia, Zimbabwe, Namibia, Tanzania, and South Africa.

As a Xhosa (a native South African ethnic group), Sontonga was denied South African citizenship by the pre-apartheid government but was allowed to work in a colonial mission school. His song, "Nkosi Sikelel' iAfrika," combines the western hymn style with indigenous South African music.

Although the song was originally written for the mission school choir, it rapidly spread throughout South African countries. It articulated the collective heartcry of black South African people during an oppressive time in their history.

This is an example of how songwriting is a vehicle to enrich the Christian community while also providing a means to express the tragedy and triumphs of our collective experience.

Missional Values

Music helps you remember stuff—and worship music helps
you remember the importance of Christ and the mission
of his church. The influence of music has a profound effect
upon our emotional responses and therefore our motivations.
This evidence is not just anecdotal. Research has proven
that music affects us psychologically and physically.

"In some sense, music can be thought of
as a delivery system for emotional content.
We do not experience music so much as
we experience ourselves experiencing music.

Our ears funnel the sound to a deeper
layer of our being, a layer where sound is
made significant. Of course, not all music
is equally effective and not every listener
is equally moved by musical stimuli. But
even the most literate musicians and
harshest critics will admit, readily or
reluctantly, that music is predominantly
about emotions. It only begins as sound."
— Jonathan L. Friedmann

Throughout church history, we see the common thread of music development alongside Christian liturgy. The power of music is that it has the ability to transmit theology and reinforce mission in a very deep and meaningful way. The Christian Reformers and revivalists of early Western church history were notable for their use of music to leverage change in biblical understanding and liturgical practices. John and Charles Wesley were especially famous for their use of songs as a way to reinforce biblical teaching in the Methodist movement. The practice of songwriting allows us to harness music to shape the culture, community, and movement of the local church.

Diversity

The history of music has shown a deep connection between community and belief. Before concerts and clubs, music was at the center of hospitality, community ceremonies, and cultural festivals. In other words, music is an expression of cultural identity and beliefs. Embedded in the Christian narrative is the idea that God's intent has always been to bless the nations through his redemptive work. When we celebrate the creative contributions of the people of God in every nation of the world, we acknowledge the sacredness and dignity with which God created all people. The Christian tradition is rich with diverse expressions of praise; a tapestry that testifies of God being honored in as many forms and in as many places as possible.

Charles Spurgeon makes an insightful comment on this idea in his famous volume on Psalms entitled *The Treasury of David*:

"'What shall I render unto the LORD for all his benefits toward me?'

The question of the verse is a very proper one: the Lord has rendered so much mercy to us that we ought to look about us, and look within us, and see what can be done by us to manifest our gratitude.

We ought not only to do what is plainly before us, but also with holy ingenuity to search out various ways by which we may render fresh praises unto our God.

His benefits are so many that we cannot number them, and our ways of acknowledging his bestowments ought to be varied and numerous in proportion. Each person should have his own peculiar mode of expressing gratitude.

The Lord sends each one a special benefit, let each one enquire, 'What shall I render? What form of service would be most becoming in me?'"

Influence and Legacy

For generations, music has not only impacted the culture of the local church but has extended beyond the Christian community into the mainstream. Music is a language that can transcend both genre and culture. Many churches have expanded their influence and extended the legacy of the church through musical expression. Hillsong, one of the most prominent music brands in Christianity, started out as a church plant in the "Hills" area of Sydney, Australia. Brian Houston, the senior pastor, encouraged the local church music ministry to write and record original songs. Over time, the musical influence of the church grew to what is now a global phenomenon. This ministry, like many other church movements, has leveraged songwriting as a tool to engage people with the gospel. The impact of these churches is survived not only by sermons and services but by songs.

CHAPTER 2
SUMMARY

SONGWRITING SHAPES THE WAY
PEOPLE ENCOUNTER GOD IN
WORSHIP AND AFFECTS THEIR
BIBLICAL UNDERSTANDING.

SONGWRITING HAS A UNIQUE
POWER TO CATALYZE THE CULTURE,
COMMUNITY, AND MOVEMENT
OF THE LOCAL CHURCH.

DIVERSE MUSICAL EXPRESSION
ACKNOWLEDGES THE SACREDNESS
AND DIGNITY WITH WHICH
GOD CREATED ALL PEOPLE.

SONGS HAVE THE ABILITY TO EXPAND
THE REACH OF THE GOSPEL.

CHAPTER 2 REFLECTION

Based upon what you read in chapters 1 and 2, what historical fact from songwriting in the local church resonated with you most? Why?

What are some practical ways you can serve the local church through your songwriting?

CHAPTER 2 WRITING PROMPT

Re-read the hymn from page 38 of this chapter:

"Nkosi sikelel' iAfrika (Lord, bless Africa)
Maluphakanyis' uphondo lwayo (May her horn rise high up)
Yiva imithandazo yethu (Hear Thou our prayers)
Nkosi sikelela, Thina lusapho lwayo (And bless us)

Yehla Moya, Yehla Moya, (Descend, O Spirit)
Yehla Moya Oyingcwele (Descend, O Holy Spirit)

Go to the writing journal section of this book on page 119. Spend at least thirty minutes writing a song that addresses an issue in your local community.

Worship is first a response
before it becomes a practice.

SECTION II.

THE CREATIVE

Objective: At the conclusion of this section, you will gain a biblical perspective on your identity as a worshipper and the relationship between creative responsibility, character, and community.

Worship songwriting is the exercise
of knowing God and skillfully
making him known through music.

CHAPTER 3:
I AM A WORSHIPPER

In the previous chapters, we took a historical look at the development of worship practice throughout church history; Moses, King David, the church fathers, and other leaders all contributing in various ways to the shaping of worship music. These leaders were defined by their devotion to God and their songs were just an extension of their lifestyle.

As worshippers and songwriters, we share the same responsibility of knowing how God wants to be worshipped and how we should communicate this to our local communities.

Foundations of Worship

"But the hour is coming, and is now here, when the true worshipers will worship the Father in spirit and truth, for the Father is seeking such people to worship him. God is spirit, and those who worship him must worship in spirit and truth."
— John 4:23–24

In this passage of scripture, Jesus tells us three important things about worship:

1. TRUE WORSHIP IS DEFINED BY GOD, NOT US.

God defines worship for us because sin has ruined our ability to clearly see and know him. We would be left groping in the dark if not for God revealing himself to us and marking off the boundaries of true worship. Jesus was the greatest worshipper to ever live. Looking into the life of Jesus gives us the best possible example of true worship. Every moment of Jesus' life was God-defined and filled with glory and honor to God the Father.

2. TRUE WORSHIP MUST BE BOTH SPIRITUAL AND TRUTHFUL.

Jesus tells us that "God is spirit" and as spirit, he cannot be limited to one specific place or time. This is important to understand because we can often make the mistake of trying to restrict the worship of God to a particular time, place, and/or experience.

Our truthfulness in worship is contingent upon our understanding of what God has revealed about himself and us in scripture. As we study and engage the Holy Spirit, he opens up our eyes to see the truth of God revealed in the person of Jesus.

3. GOD IS SEEKING TRUE WORSHIPPERS WHO WILL ENGAGE HIM AS HE HAS DEFINED.

To be clear, God's search for worshippers does not begin with his need to be worshipped, but with our need to worship him. The power of true worship is that we are transformed as we are ushered into a deeper understanding of who God is, what he does, and who we were created to be.

God does not require that true worshippers be charismatic, musical, or creative people. Above all else, he is seeking those whose hearts will be completely surrendered to him.

Regulative Principle vs Normative Principle:

"The **Regulative Principle** of worship teaches that the public worship of God should include ONLY those elements that are instituted, commanded, or appointed by command of example in the Bible.

In other words, it is the belief that God institutes in scripture whatever he requires for worship in the Church, and everything else should be avoided . . ."

The **Normative Principle** of worship teaches that whatever is not prohibited in scripture is PERMITTED in worship, so long as it is agreeable to the peace and unity of the church.

In other words, there must be agreement with the general practice of the Church and no prohibition in Scripture for whatever is done in public worship."

— Pastor Paul Barker, Crafting a Theology of Worship

God is **transcendent**. He is above and beyond his creation and exists independent of it. Because God is transcendent, worship should be majestic, awe-inspiring, and reverent . . . Because God is immanent, worship should be relaxed, uninhibited, and easy going."

— Pastor Paul Barker, Crafting a Theology of Worship

"I appeal to you therefore, brothers, by the mercies of God, to present your bodies as a living sacrifice, holy and acceptable to God, which is your spiritual worship. Do not be conformed to this world, but be transformed by the renewal of your mind, that by testing you may discern what is the will of God, what is good and acceptable and perfect."
— Romans 12:1–2

The Worshipper

Even though God does not require creativity to be a true worshipper, he has gifted many of us with creative abilities. Unfortunately, as creative people, our sense of identity as worshippers is too often derived from our skills and abilities. Maybe you've asked yourself one of the following questions after a worship service: *Did I sing the song well? Will people think my song is good? Did anyone hear that cool riff I did?* These questions are helpful in assessing the development of our skills but we can mistakenly view the answers as indicators of our overall value.

God does not see us this way. We are not performance machines; we are people made in his image and likeness with intrinsic value.

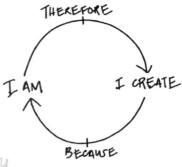

"Religion teaches us that our function determines our worth and our identity (I am because I do). Worship teaches us that our identity determines our worth and our function (I do because I am). And God determines our identity."
— Zach Neese

Worship is first a response before it becomes a practice.

BEING ⟶ DOING
(arrow back from DOING to BEING)

This truth is vitally important because once the issue of identity is settled, we are free to create without fear of our value being compromised. In the most simple terms, our role as creative people, like every other person is "to glorify [i.e. worship] God and enjoy him forever."

The Worship Songwriter

"My heart overflows with a pleasing theme; I address my verses to the king; my tongue is like the pen of a ready scribe."
— Psalm 45:1

It's also important to remember that God will always be greater than anything we ever write about him.

The Apostle Paul said it this way:

"Oh, the depth of the riches and wisdom and knowledge of God! How unsearchable are his judgments and how inscrutable his ways!" - Romans 11:33

The above passage is both humbling and inspiring. It is humbling in the sense that God is unfathomably more great than our attempts to describe him. It is inspiring in the sense that we will never run dry of ways to experience and describe his greatness.

Worship songwriting is the exercise of knowing God and skillfully making him known through music. A song provides a medium for people to absorb and recall deep truths concerning the Christian faith. Therefore, songwriting should employ lyric and melody to expertly guide God's people in worship.

Consider this:

OUR MOTIVATION FOR SONGWRITING IS AS IMPORTANT AS THE SONGS WE WRITE.

God gives us gifts to expand his platform, not our own. In Mark 10:17–27, Jesus has a conversation with a rich young guy about this very subject. Here's what Jesus said to him in verse 21: "You lack one thing: go, sell all that you have and give to the poor, and you will have treasure in heaven; and come, follow me."

In other words, "get rid of your platform, and I will give you mine." What Jesus said was simple but not easy. Unfortunately, this guy was unwilling to give up his empire. Too often, we find ourselves unwilling to sacrifice our idea of a platform, not realizing that it's temporary. We should continue to write songs and be creative. We should seek to be innovative and inspired in what we do. We should be diligent, growing confident in the fact that hard work carries its own form of influence. However, we must do it all for the glory of God. Remember, the greatest platform any of us could possibly attain will be the one upon which we stand and hear God say, "Well done."

CHAPTER 3 SUMMARY

GOD LOOKS FOR WORSHIPPERS WHO WILL WORSHIP HIM AS HE HAS DEFINED, IN SPIRIT AND TRUTH.

OUR ROLE AS CREATIVE PEOPLE, LIKE EVERY OTHER PERSON IS "TO GLORIFY [I.E. WORSHIP] GOD AND ENJOY HIM FOREVER."

AS SONGWRITERS, OUR GIFTS AND SKILLS ARE USEFUL IN SHAPING THE VOCABULARY OF WORSHIP IN THE CHURCH BUT MOST IMPORTANTLY, TO EXPRESS OUR PERSONAL DEVOTION TO GOD.

CHAPTER 3 REFLECTION

Revisit the questionnaire we provided on page 8. Based on your answers, fill in the Songwriting Self-Assessment below:

SONGWRITING SELF-ASSESSMENT

1. **Collaboration:** on a scale of 1 to 5, how comfortable do you feel writing in community?

Awkward   1   2   3   4   5   **Super comfy**

What are three practical steps you can take to improve?

2. **Effectiveness:** on a scale of 1 to 5, how often do you receive positive feedback on your songs?

Never   1   2   3   4   5   **Quite often**

What are three practical steps you can take to improve?

3. **Personal Devotion:** on a scale of 1 to 5, how much has your songwriting affected your devotional intimacy?

Very little   1   2   3   4   5   Significantly

What are 3 practical steps you can take to improve?

4. **Consistency:** on a scale of 1 to 5, how often do you write worship songs?

Never   1   2   3   4   5   Quite often

What are three practical steps you can take to improve?

5. **Ministry:** on a scale of 1 to 5, how deeply does songwriting affect your ministry?

Never   1   2   3   4   5   Quite often

What are three practical steps you can take to improve?

SONGWRITING GOALS

Based on your answers from the Songwriting Self-Assessment, what goals do you want to accomplish by the end of this workbook?

CHAPTER 3
WRITING PROMPT

Go to the writing journal section of this book on page 119. Spend at least thirty minutes writing a song based on the following Bible verse:

"For we are his workmanship, created in Christ Jesus for good works, which God prepared beforehand, that we should walk in them."
— Ephesians 2:10

One of the skills of a great songwriter
is being able to place themselves and
the listener into the story of the song.

CHAPTER 4: CREATE RESPONSIBLY

Now that you know what worship is and how you can worship through your songwriting, the groundwork is laid for you to improve your skill and grow in creative community. Being creatively responsible is critical to your growth as a songwriter. Learning to be consistent, accountable, and generous are a few of the disciplines we will cover in this chapter.

Skill Development

Understanding who we are as worshippers provides a firm foundation upon which we can build our skills. We each have a sacred responsibility to consistently put our gifts to use in an effort to develop skills that honor God. The most prolific and impactful songwriters in church history did not stumble upon their influence. Even if they were not looking to be famous, oftentimes their songs gained recognition by virtue of their diligence.

"Do you see a man skillful in his work? He will stand before kings; he will not stand before obscure men."
— Proverbs 22:29.

Here are some key best practices when developing your songwriting skills:

CONSISTENCY IS KEY.

Write a little every day and keep a notebook of ideas. An important practice in finding your voice as a songwriter is writing on a regular basis. Putting together words, clarifying thoughts, and developing a knack for rhyme scheme will give your songwriting polish and lyrical sophistication.

BE A LEARNER.

Be a student of music. Begin listening to the kinds of songs you want to write. There is an old adage in music that you must "imitate before you innovate." Knowing the rules of songwriting will give you a better sense of when it's appropriate to break them. It's also important that you expand your musical creativity by exploring other styles. Reading books and attending workshops and classes are also great ways to expand your musical knowledge base.

HAVE A PLAN.

Revisit your songwriting goals from the last chapter. When starting a song think about who, what, when, where, and why. One of the skills of a great songwriter is being able to place themselves and the listener into the story of the song. Another fancy word for this is vicariousness. This is an invaluable tool in helping your audience to connect with your song. Below are three potential contexts for your song:

Personal: It's important that every worshipper take time alone with God to be refreshed, encouraged, and inspired. In these moments, our hearts are stirred with affection and devotion. However, it's important to recognize that some songs should remain between you and God.

Congregational: Some songs will be the result of inspiration and/or direction from our local church leaders. We must embrace the fact that these songs may not extend beyond our local church.

Ecumenical: Some songs inspire the nations to unify in praise and adoration of the one true God. We might call these songs "rare" in that they transcend personal preference and congregational specificity to penetrate into all of the world.

EDIT YOUR SONGS.

A solid best practice is to embrace the idea that a song is not finished until it is revised and/or rewritten. Too often we can over-spiritualize the songwriting process with "God gave me . . . " and end up missing out on more potent lyrical and melodic content. As a songwriter, it's important not to settle for a song that simply feels good to you.

Here are some tips for boosting your song-editing process:

"A writer's best friend is the waste paper basket." —Isaac Bashevis Singer

Rewrite, rewrite, rewrite: Remove unnecessary words or phrases. Ask a friend/mentor to identify the strongest part of your song. Consider rewriting the other sections to match the lyrical and melodic strength of that part. Make sure that all songwriters in your group agree on changes to your song.

Get feedback: Allow a few trusted friends/mentors to listen to your song before sharing it publicly. First impressions are important. Take care to fine-tune your song's arrangement with a skilled musician or producer. Your song deserves to be featured in the best way possible. Anonymously preview the song to your congregation. Afterward, ask a few people to give their reaction to the song.

Live to write another day: Give yourself some time away from the song before you decide to finalize it. You may determine, after some thought and feedback, that the song is not worth completing; don't be afraid to trash it and/or start over.

Co-Writing and Generosity

You may have noticed in previous chapters that we've mentioned the value of community and diversity as it relates to songwriting. One of the most effective ways to grow in your songwriting skill is to write with others—especially those who are more experienced. Because co-writing is such a vulnerable experience, it's important to set borders that allow for creativity to flow and relationships to remain intact.

DEVELOP RELATIONSHIP

"Behold, how good and pleasant it is when brothers dwell in unity! . . . For there the LORD has commanded the blessing, life forevermore."
— Psalm 133:1,3

Every writer has a unique personal story that is important to the songwriting process. Ask your co-writer(s) questions to get the creative process started. Here are a few examples: *What is God doing in your life? What's happening in your local church? What kind of music do you like?*

BE VULNERABLE.

Discuss your strengths and weaknesses as a writer. You may discover that you and your co-writer(s) have complementary skills which will help your song develop.

Create a "No Diva" zone. There are no bad ideas, only better ones. Make sure to respect the contributions of your fellow co-writer(s), but also be open to constructive feedback.

Be willing to write with people and/or in a style that is not comfortable. You may discover that you have a skill in a particular style of music that you otherwise wouldn't have realized on your own.

COMMUNITY > SONGS

Co-writing is as much about relationships as it is writing great songs. It could be argued that writing alone is easier. However, as inconvenient or uncomfortable as co-writing may be to some, there are hidden benefits to collaboration; these include learning to give and receive feedback, accountability and mentorship, and access to different points of view, to name a few.

BE GENEROUS.

As music expands from the community into the commercial sphere, the discussion of biblical generosity becomes increasingly important. If you're a songwriter, you've probably heard horror stories about plagiarism and copyright infringement. Every argument over songwriting copyright began with an exchange of ideas. This is why it's so important to make biblical generosity a practice of collaborative songwriting. The following passage of scripture gives us some insight into the kind of attitude we should seek to cultivate as co-writers:

Fun fact: According to CCLI.com, the most popular worship songs sung in churches today are all co-written.

"In the morning sow your seed, and at evening withhold not your hand, for you do not know which will prosper, this or that, or whether both alike will be good."
— Ecclesiastes 11:6

There are three basic principles in this passage that should inform how we handle the both the sharing of ideas and songwriting credit:

"It is best to enter into a business negotiation as a prosperous soul and not as a victim. Prosperity attracts. Neediness repels."
— Malcolm Du Plessis

Sow your talent diligently. God wants us to be attentive and persistent as co-writers.

Sow your talent liberally. God wants us to share our musical talent with the local church, not withhold it.

God wants us to be satisfied in knowing that he will prosper us in time.

CO-WRITING BEST PRACTICES

1. **Schedule time:** Make songwriting a priority by setting a calendar date for at least a two (2)- to three (3)- hour session.

2. **Discuss "splits" beforehand:** "Splits" is a term that refers to the percentage of copyright ownership of each writer. (A complete song is equal to 100%).

3. **Bring Your Own Content:** As a songwriter, be armed with topics, scriptures, melodies, etc. before going into a songwriting session.

4. **Record your ideas:** Use journals, voice memos, and other apps to capture your songwriting process.

5. **Finish songs:** Set a goal. Make a commitment to complete a song before you start writing another one. Find two or three people with whom you have songwriting chemistry. Some people are better "song-starters" and others are better "song-finishers."

CHAPTER 4 SUMMARY

WE EACH HAVE A SACRED RESPONSIBILITY TO CONSISTENTLY PUT OUR GIFTS TO USE IN AN EFFORT TO DEVELOP SKILLS THAT HONOR GOD.

ONE OF THE MOST EFFECTIVE WAYS TO GROW IN YOUR SONGWRITING SKILL IS TO WRITE WITH OTHERS.

APPROACH CO-WRITING WITH THE MINDSET OF GENEROSITY AND RELATIONSHIP DEVELOPMENT.

CHAPTER 4 REFLECTION

From the reading, which skill-development best practice do you struggle with most? What are some ways you can improve in this area?

CHAPTER 4
WRITING PROMPT

Go to the writing journal section of this book on page 119. Grab a couple friends or strangers and schedule a two-hour collaborative writing session this week. Here's a guideline for your songwriting group:

STEP 1: Get to know your co-writers.

Ask some simple questions like:

- *What scriptures have been resonating with you?*
- *Give a testimony of how God has impacted your life.*
- *What aspects of songwriting do you enjoy most?*
- *What kind of music do you listen to?*

STEP 2: Start your song.

Here are a few practical ways to start a song:

- Read scripture.
- Pray together.
- Play your instrument and vocalize (make melody).
- Choose an idea out of your connect time.
- See if someone already has an idea.

STEP 3: Write your song.

STEP 4: Record and share a demo to the group.

STEP 5: Schedule a time to edit your song.

Our songs should unveil
the gospel, not obscure it.

SECTION III.

THE CRAFT

Objective: At the end of this section, you will know how to employ the parts of a song, melody, and lyric to craft a musically pleasing song.

Great songs are most
defined by the effectiveness
of their choruses.

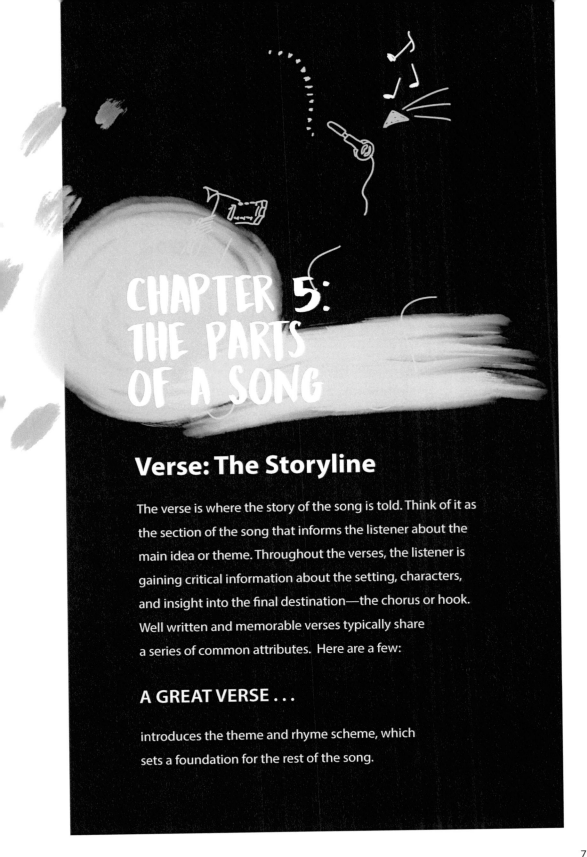

CHAPTER 5: THE PARTS OF A SONG

Verse: The Storyline

The verse is where the story of the song is told. Think of it as the section of the song that informs the listener about the main idea or theme. Throughout the verses, the listener is gaining critical information about the setting, characters, and insight into the final destination—the chorus or hook. Well written and memorable verses typically share a series of common attributes. Here are a few:

A GREAT VERSE . . .

introduces the theme and rhyme scheme, which sets a foundation for the rest of the song.

"Each verse, or A section, acts like a scene in a play or a chapter in a book. The effect is like looking at a piece of panel art made up of separate screens. Each screen is a scene. Taken together, they tell a story."
— Robert Sterling

employs literary devices such as alliteration or imagery to reinforce the main idea.

creates an intriguing flow of thought that can only be satisfied by the chorus.

Chorus: The "Aha" Moment

A strong second verse sheds new light on the chorus idea. Challenge yourself to approach your storyline in a different way the second time around. Even if the chorus is the same, the listener should experience it differently as the song progresses.

The chorus is the climax of the songwriter's story. If the lyrical theme of the song is like a bull's eye, the chorus is the part of the song that hits the target most directly. The goal of every chorus should be to unveil the lyrical theme in a way that memorably engages the emotions and imagination of the listener.

Since the chorus is typically the focal point of every song it usually contains the lyrical hook or title. Most commonly, the lyrical hook or title of the song is introduced in the first or last line of the chorus. Great songs are most defined by the effectiveness of their chorus.

SOME FEATURES OF GREAT CHORUSES ARE ...

strong melodic and/or lyrical repetition.

binding together the details of the verses into a culminating thought.

typically repeated in the same way throughout the song with little or no variation.

Bridge: The Plot Twist

If you think of a song as a story, the bridge is the plot twist. It serves as a melodic and sometimes lyrical deviation from the cycle of verses and choruses in a song. A bridge can add intensity and tension to a song or serve as breathing space in between intense verses and choruses. When listening to a song, the way you can tell you've arrived at the bridge is that it doesn't sound like anything else. A great bridge uses contrast in melody to perk the listeners' ears up and add interest. Lyrically, it is a great space to explain a new aspect of your song's main idea or reinforce the lyrical theme in a new way.

A GREAT BRIDGE …

adds dynamic contrast toward the end of the song.

embellishes the song theme in a way the chorus doesn't.

never distracts from the chorus.

However, just as not all stories need plot twists, not all songs need bridges. If you're trying to decide if your song needs a bridge, ask yourself: *Does the song seem finished? Am I getting bored near the end of my song? Do my ears need a break from the tension in the verses and choruses? Do I need to add a song section to raise the stakes?* If you answer yes to any of these questions, it may be time to write a bridge.

Pre-Chorus: The Guide

In song arrangement, instrumental turns/ channels are commonly used to melodically introduce new sections of a song, typically used before the verse and/or bridge.

The pre-chorus has many names: lift, lead-in, turn, channel, or climb. Whatever you call it, the pre-chorus serves one purpose—to guide the listener from the verse to the chorus.

A pre-chorus shouldn't have a personality of its own. It's the sidekick, written to support the stars of the song—the verse and chorus. It's typically a couple lines long and can either reinforce the key line of the song or introduce the chorus. The pre-chorus functions well when it complements the sections it sits between, smoothing the transition from one thought to another.

A GREAT PRE-CHORUS ...

is short.

provides a preview of the chorus' content.

isn't necessary to good song form—proceed with caution.

CHAPTER 5 SUMMARY

THE VERSE IS WHERE THE
STORY OF THE SONG IS TOLD.

THE GOAL OF EVERY CHORUS
SHOULD BE TO UNVEIL THE THEME
IN A WAY THAT MEMORABLY
ENGAGES THE EMOTIONS AND
IMAGINATION OF THE LISTENER.

THE BRIDGE SERVES AS A MELODIC
AND SOMETIMES LYRICAL
DEVIATION FROM THE CYCLE OF
VERSES AND CHORUSES IN A SONG.

THE PRE-CHORUS SERVES TO
GUIDE THE LISTENER FROM
THE VERSE TO THE CHORUS.

CHAPTER 5
REFLECTION

What part of a song is most difficult for you to write? What can
you apply from this chapter to improve on your skill?

CHAPTER 5
WRITING PROMPT

Go to the writing journal section of this book on page 119. Take thirty minutes to

pick a weak section from a song you've already written, and do some revisions.

As a musical storyteller, it's important that you are knowledgeable and skilled in using the full range of language.

CHAPTER 6: LYRICAL TOOLS

Theme, biblical accuracy, and poetic devices are fundamental to every song. In this chapter we will give you tools to develop your wordplay and lyrical vocabulary.

Lyrical Foundations

THEOLOGY

Theology is the study of God's nature and God's nature is most clearly revealed to us through Scripture in the life of Christ. Theologically sound songs are the end result of filtering our lyrics through the Christ-centered lens of Scripture. When we mix good theology with life experience, we write songs that personally connect people with the story of God.

EMOTIONAL SINCERITY

Songs written with emotional sincerity will spark heartfelt responses to God in worship. While solid theology connects people to the story of God, the sincerity of a lyric connects people to the heart of God.

ESTABLISHING THEME

Theme, also known as concept, can be described as the "bull's eye" of a song. All lyrical content should support the theme of your song, or it should try to hit the "bull's eye." Starting with the Bible is a great way to find a strong theme. Scripture is filled with topics and ideas that revolve around the personhood, character, and attributes of God. Another way to find a powerful song theme is to reflect upon a significant life experience in light of the gospel message. After you've established your theme, get to the point! Communicate your theme or concept quickly, keeping in mind that the average listener will give a song about thirty seconds before he or she "checks out." Remember, the point of your song is unknown to your listeners until it is clearly expressed.

Literary Devices

As a musical storyteller, it's important that you are knowledgeable and skilled in using the full range of language. Songs are a form of literature although we often don't think of them in that way. Many of the same literary tools employed by your favorite author are important to songwriting.

The following devices are especially common to songwriting and useful in focusing the attention of the listener.

ALLITERATION

Words that repeat the same sound—usually consonants. Example: Ally alligator ate Alex.

IMAGERY

Words that paint pictures in your mind.
Example: "The Old Rugged Cross"

PERSONIFICATION

Treating a place, thing, or idea like a person.
Example: The trees sing for joy.

SIMILE

A comparison using the word "like" or "as."
Example: His heart as deep as the sea.

METAPHOR

A comparison when one thing is called something else. Example: Your love is a river.

ANAPHORA

Words that are repeated at the start of lines. This is very common in songwriting. Example: how deep, how wide, how great is your love for me.

Cliches and Christianese

Spending time with like-minded people is unavoidable in church culture. We serve the same God, read the same Bible, and have shared worship practices for centuries. You can see how we end up using the same words all the time. This is why common Christian phrases should be used infrequently as they can become cliche.

"Cliches are other people's licks. They don't come from your emotions . . . They are familiar—maybe uncomfortably familiar."
— Pat Pattison

Some examples of common church words and phrases:

- The battle is raging
- Even when I can't see
- One thing I know
- In the midnight hour
- You spoke a word
- Death has lost its sting
- Trials and tribulations
- At (upon) the cross
- You('ve) won the victory
- Washed in the blood
- Your glory and majesty

- Be lifted high

- I am yours

- Your love never fails

- We are your sons and daughters

- Rain down on me (us)

- Pour out your love (your love poured out)

If you've noticed, the above phrases have been used in some of the most popular Christian songs of all time. However, in most cases, they were used for the first time or in a fresh way when those songs were written. This list is not to condemn or criticize the use of these phrases but to remind us of how easy it is for popular phrases to become cliche.

The same is true of "church words," also known as "christianese." Many of the words that hold great meaning and power for believers are of little value or importance to people who are unbelievers or unchurched. Christian worship has historically focused on the gathering of believers and should maintain a sense of reverence and biblical substance. However, as songwriters, it is important that we find new ways to communicate old truths that both strengthen our core beliefs while also bringing clarity to those who may be new to the faith. Our songs should unveil the gospel, not obscure it.

Rhyme

Much like song form, rhyme is a foundational building block of songwriting. The effective use of rhyme is often the determining factor of whether a song is memorable or mundane. To be clear, not all rhymes are created equal; good ones mesmerize us and bad ones make us skip the song.

A SIMPLE DEFINITION OF RHYME IS TWO OR MORE WORDS THAT CORRESPOND IN SOUND. WITHIN THE CONTEXT OF SONGWRITING, RHYMING IS USED TO CREATE PATTERNS OF SOUNDS THAT CONNECT PHRASES TOGETHER.

Rhymes come in all shapes and sizes—some are more obvious than others. Here are a few of the most commonly used types of rhyme in songwriting:

PERFECT RHYME

Words that share the same vowel and final consonant sounds. Example: grace, place, chase, race.

NEAR RHYME

Words that almost rhyme (also known as "slant" or "imperfect rhyme"). Example: prove-rule or love-dust.

INTERNAL RHYME

Rhymes that happen in the sentence rather than
at the end. Example: He made a way for us.

We could say that the above rhyme types fall along a spectrum
of extroverted to introverted. A perfect rhyme begs for our
attention. The near rhyme subtly waves hello. While the
internal rhyme plays peek-a-boo throughout the line.
Keep in mind that the rhyme type will affect the
scansion of your song; therefore, rhyme should always
be used to emphasize important words or ideas.

Each line of a song has a particular way of lyrically reinforcing
the main idea. Rhyme scheme is a pattern of lines that creates
an organized repetition of sounds. If a rhyme type organizes the
sounds in each line, a rhyme scheme organizes each line into a
stanza. Rhyme type is to word as rhyme scheme is to sentence.

We've chosen to give examples of rhyme scheme by using
lowercase letters to represent lines with corresponding sounds.

"To ignore the rhyming demands of the
melody is to weaken the power of the song."
— Robert Sterling

S

ALTERNATE RHYME (abab)

*Common in Pop/
CCM/Gospel
songwriting styles*

"Lord I Lift Your Name On High" by Rick Founds

"Lord I lift your name on high (near rhyme: a),

Lord I love to sing your praises (near rhyme: b),

I'm so glad you're in my life (near rhyme: a),

I'm so glad you came to save us (near rhyme: b)."

COUPLET (aa, bb, cc)

*Commonly used in the
refrain sections of songs*

"El Shaddai" Amy Grant

"El Shaddai, El Shaddai (perfect rhyme: a)

Er-elyon na Adonai (perfect rhyme: a)

Age to Age, you're still the same (perfect rhyme: b)

By the power of your name (perfect rhyme: b)."

TRIPLET (aaa, bbb, ccc)

"Christ the Solid Rock" by Edward Mote

"On Christ the Solid Rock I stand (near rhyme: a),

All other ground is sinking sand (near rhyme: a)

All other ground is sinking sand (perfect rhyme: a)."

ENCLOSED RHYME (abba)

"Fire Burns" by Jon Owens

"Your fire (perfect rhyme: a)
Burn within me (perfect rhyme: b)
Burn within me (perfect rhyme: b)
With your fire (perfect rhyme: a)."

BALLAD/QUATRAIN (abcb)

"O Mighty One" by Justin Gray

"To you I bow, O Mighty One (no rhyme: a)
For you are high upon the throne (near rhyme: b)
Let all the people stand in awe (no rhyme: c)
Of love and mercy you have shown (near rhyme: b)."

Dos & Don'ts of Lyric Writing

DO'S Challenge the trends. If you're hearing too many songs with water references, write about fire!

Write with your church in mind.

Identify a style and genre for your song. This helps to focus your songwriting and give you a musical framework.

Find the balance between positivity and pain in your storytelling. God's message of hope and redemption is essential to the storyline of every worship song.

Do your homework. Make sure your lyrics aren't already someone else's lyrics.

DON'TS Avoid homophones at the end of your rhyming sentences.

Don't overuse unfamiliar words. Nobody likes a smartypants!

Don't prioritize rhyme over lyrical substance.

Over-extended metaphors are like bad jokes; they should have stopped a long time ago.

Don't write a "run-on" song. There's a reason why the typical song length is three to five minutes.

CHAPTER 6
SUMMARY

GOOD LYRICS ARE
THEOLOGICALLY SOUND AND
SINCERE WITH A STRONG THEME.

COMMON CHRISTIAN PHRASES
SHOULD BE USED INFREQUENTLY
AS THEY CAN BECOME CLICHE.

THE EFFECTIVE USE OF RHYME
IS OFTEN THE DETERMINING
FACTOR OF WHETHER A SONG IS
MEMORABLE OR MUNDANE.

CHAPTER 6
REFLECTION

What inspires or challenges you about writing lyrics? Why?

CHAPTER 6
WRITING PROMPT

Go to the writing journal section of this book on page 119. Spend at least
thirty minutes writing a song using an unfamiliar rhyme scheme.

"Music has the power to stop
time, but music also keeps time."
—Questlove

CHAPTER 7: MELODY, HARMONY, & RHYTHM

"Melody + Harmony + Rhythm = Music"
— Robert Sterling

Together, melody, harmony, and rhythm serve as the audible illustration of the lyric and help to place the listener into the story of the song. Great songwriters find ways to employ these three elements with nuance and expertise.

Melody

Melody is made up of a pattern of sounds expressed with repetition, variation, and contrast. These three components help us differentiate between the sections of a song and determine the shape of the overall composition.

REPETITION

In the Bible, Jesus would often use repetition to underscore a major point. It's much the same in songwriting. If our goal is to engage the listener and make our song memorable, it's important for us to master the skill of melodic repetition. Unlimited access to music has raised the stakes for songwriters to make sticky songs. Skillful use of repetition drives the melodic point home and causes songs to get stuck in listeners' heads. All this to say, if you want to write a catchy tune, use repetition.

Example:

"It Is Well With My Soul" by Horatio Spafford

Repetition of melody between "it is well" and "with my soul"

It is well, with my soul. It is well, it is well with my soul.

VARIATION

A simple definition of melodic variation is "a melodic
line repeated in an altered form." Great songwriters
know when to make smart departures from what is
expected without throwing the listener off. Tweaking
a phrase melodically can be just enough to unlock the
next door you want your listener to walk through.

Example:

"Many Waters" by Jon Owens, Chris Davis, & Robrt Ellis, Jr.

*Slight variation in
the ascending scales
for "Lord Almigthy"
and "to the king"*

For the Lord Almighty reigns. To the king most

ho - ly.   To the Lamb so worthy...

*Repetition of melody
between "most holy"
and "so worthy" &
between "to the king"
and "to the Lamb"*

"When the variation is extreme enough, a
true departure from the phrases preceding
it, the variation becomes a contrast."
— Robert Sterling

CONTRAST

Melodic contrast is placing two opposing melodic lines closely together. It helps to distinguish between sections of a song. In order for the listener to know when a song is shifting from the verse to the chorus, there needs to be a distinct contrast in the melody. There is a fine line between good melodic contrast and contrast that is too abrupt. This is like yanking the steering wheel while your listener is cruising along in the song. Great tools to soften melodic contrast are the use of pre-choruses, channels, and instrumentals.

Example:

"Fill Us Up (Pour Us Out)" by James Murrell, Kristin Hill, Justin Chapman, & Shayne Hill

fill us up   pour us out   to be your hands and feet oh Lord

Ho-ly   Spi-rit   draw me near.

Vocal Range:

In Nashville, even the coffee baristas have incredible vocal range. So you might get away with writing and performing vocally challenging songs. But for the rest of us who live on planet earth, the average untrained singer is only capable of singing within about one octave range. Therefore, if you want to write a song for a congregation of non-singers, keep it within one octave.

Contrast between the verse and chorus creates a sense of tension and release.

MELODIC PATTERNS

We use repetition, variation, and contrast to create melodic patterns in songs. These patterns center around one musical idea or motif, usually functioning as the chorus or refrain. All of the other musical elements work together to support that melodic motif.

Melodic Pattern Best Practices

MAKE A CHANGE.

Many great songs have soaring melodies in the chorus which provides a strong contrast between song sections. This is one way of using contrast to bring new life to the melody of your song.

TWIST THE MUSICAL PHRASE.

Use variation and/or repetition to create interest. If your verses have a busy melody, it might help to make the melody of your chorus short and repetitive.

STAY THE COURSE.

The melodies of all verses should be repeated. Choruses are the "glue." The chorus or refrain melody should be the stickiest. The more repetitive the melody, the stickier it gets.

SYNCOPATION IS YOUR FRIEND.

Offbeat and unexpected rhythmic patterns can spice up your composition and be a welcomed change of scenery for your listener.

Text painting is using melody and rhythm to mimic the lyrics of the song. For example, in "The Beat" (Every Nation Music), the chorus line "it beats, it beats, we can hear it calling" uses melody and rhythm to imitate the pulse of a heartbeat.

Harmony

CHORDS

It's important to understand the function of chords without neglecting the importance of the melody. A great song employs chords to emphasize the melody.

When choosing chords to accompany your melody, make sure your melody note matches the chord.

Chord inversions and extensions can be used to add flavor to your chord progressions. Extensions can be useful for fitting melody notes into chord progressions that wouldn't otherwise match. Inversions help to highlight different notes in the chord and can add more range to the progression. So try experimenting with extensions and flipping your chord structures around.

Scale Degrees for key of C:

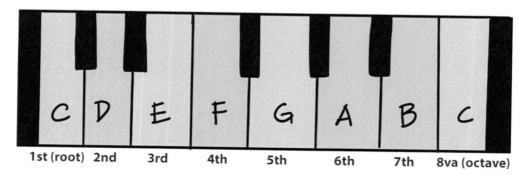

| 1st (root) | 2nd | 3rd | 4th | 5th | 6th | 7th | 8va (octave) |

Key:
Blue = notes in the C Major chord (1st, 3rd, 5th, 8va)
Pink = possible extension notes to add to the C Major Chord. These notes are included in the C Major Scale. (2nd, 3rd, 6th, 7th)

Key: pink = melody line, blue = chords

TONALITY

The relationship between the melody and the chord creates a sense of tension and release for the listener. In musical terms, we would call this tonality. In order to simplify this concept, we've provided a visual scale to help you color your melody with tone.

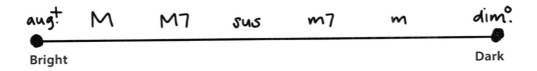

Tone Spectrum
This visual shows several chord variations on a scale from bright chords to dark chords. Chords on the brighter side are great for creating a sense of release while chords on the darker side can create a sense of tension for the listener depending on how the they are arranged in your song.

RHYTHM

"Music has the power to stop time, but music also keeps time."
— Questlove

Rhythm is essential to song composition. It's like the glue that holds the foundation of a song together. More specifically, rhythm is the pattern of pulses caused by strong and weak melodic and harmonic beats—emphasis on pattern. These patterns are used to structure a melody in time and create a pulsing sensation, known commonly as "groove."

Scansion *is the discipline of making sure that the emphasized beats of your music work naturally with the accents of your lyrics.*

To make a groove, you need meter and tempo. An easy way to understand these concepts is to think of the human heart. When you are standing still your pulse is slower than when you are running. The pulse in your body is typically an indicator of movement. In a similar way, meter and tempo are like the heartbeat of a song. Tempo is how fast your heart beats and meter is your heartbeat pattern. Whether fast or slow, the beat affects the way you respond to music. It also emphasizes certain melodic and lyrical content within a musical phrase.

CHAPTER 7 SUMMARY

GOOD MELODIES
EMPLOY REPETITION,
VARIATION, AND CONTRAST WELL.

IF THE MELODY IS THE MEAT, THEN
THE CHORD IS THE SEASONING.

RHYTHM IS LIKE THE
GLUE THAT HOLDS THE
FOUNDATION OF A SONG TOGETHER.

CHAPTER 7
REFLECTION

Use the Tone Spectrum on page 103 to write a song. Feel the rhythm and clap along to your favorite songs and feel how each one is different. Look for differences in tempo, meter, and melodic/lyrical emphasis.

CHAPTER 7
WRITING PROMPT

Go to the writing journal section of this book on page 119. Spend
at least thirty minutes writing a song to a rhythmic beat.

The interplay between verse and chorus creates a satisfying balance between melody and lyric.

CHAPTER 8: PUTTING IT ALL TOGETHER

"People have an unconscious need for symmetry and the repetition of rhyme, melody, and form satisfies that need."
— John Braheny

Song form, otherwise known as song structure, is: "The arrangement of sections in a song to contrast similar and different sections. Often, letters are used to represent different parts of a given selection: ABA, AABA, ABACA, etc" (www.musicoutfitters.com). In this chapter, we will explore two of the most common song forms and their variations.

Verse-Chorus Form

The Verse-Chorus song form spans the spectrum of music composition from Miriam Makeba to All Sons & Daughters and beyond. This song form is probably the most commonly used in popular Christian worship music today. An extremely accessible songwriting template, the verse and chorus break the theme of the song down into bite-sized pieces. The interplay between verse and chorus creates a satisfying balance between melody and lyric. Here are some variations of the Verse-Chorus song form with examples from our catalog:

Verse-Chorus-Verse-Chorus-Chorus (ABABB)

Example: **"We Stand In Awe"** by Pierre Smith, Sean Bennetts, & Sumari Schoeman

Focuses on repetition of the chorus

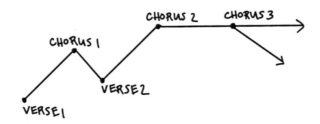

Verse-Chorus-Verse-Chorus-Bridge-Chorus (ABABCB)

Example: **"All I'm After"** by Bryson Breakey, Elizabeth Broocks, Isa Fabregas, and Rebecca Simmons

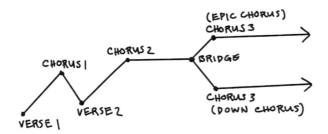

More musically dynamic/ added contrast

Verse-Pre-Chorus-Chorus-Verse-Pre-Chorus-Chorus (ABCABC)

Example: **"Radiant"** by Ashley Brooks, Bryson Breakey, Forest Martin, and Miata Jones

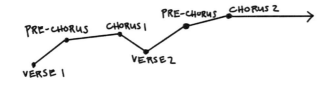

Raising the stakes before each chorus

Verse-Verse-Chorus-Verse-Chorus (AABAB)

Example: **"Heart Open Wide"** by Aaron Lucas, Joel Ramsey, Justin Gray, Lee Simon Brown, and Victor Asuncion

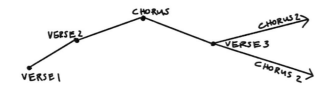

Added suspense into chorus

AAA Form

The AAA song form, also known as hymn style, is distinguished from the verse chorus form by its use of stanzas. Stanzas are the equivalent of squeezing a verse and chorus into one section. Each stanza provides new information about the theme and either opens or concludes with a refrain. The refrain is used as the lyrical/melodic hook and typically is consistent throughout the song, sometimes with some minor variations but always revealing the theme. This form is heavily reliant on great lyrical content and use of storytelling.

Example: **"O Mighty One"** by Justin Gray

VERSE + REFRAIN

VERSE + REFRAIN

VERSE + REFRAIN

Writing in AAA form means more focus on lyrical craftsmanship and more pressure to express the main idea of a song with fewer opportunities. For this form to work, you have to nail the stanza every time.

CHAPTER 8 SUMMARY

SONG FORM IS THE ARRANGEMENT OF SONG SECTIONS IN A SONG TO CONTRAST SIMILAR AND DIFFERENT SECTIONS.

THE VERSE-CHORUS SONG FORM IS PROBABLY THE MOST COMMONLY USED IN POPULAR CHRISTIAN WORSHIP MUSIC TODAY.

IN AAA FORM, STANZAS ARE THE EQUIVALENT OF SQUEEZING A VERSE AND CHORUS INTO ONE SECTION.

CHAPTER 8 REFLECTION

Identify the song forms for three of your favorite songs. How does song form help make these songs memorable to you?

CHAPTER 8
WRITING PROMPT

Go to the writing journal section of this book on page 119. Choose an unfamiliar
song form from this chapter and spend thirty minutes writing a song.

CONCLUSION

Songwriting plays an important role in church worship. God has given you, as a songwriter, the ability to articulate what he is doing in your life and in the context of your community. Each of us should rise up to become contributors in the story that God is telling through the church.

"If God is real amongst us, we should rise above our inferiority complex that pushes us to only sing songs from a few artists. Even if our songs are terrible we should still write them."
— Malcolm Du Plessis

Continue your songwriting journey. Continue to build community and explore diverse musical expressions of worship. You have the tools—now use them. Write more songs.

Play, Write, Sing,

Justin Gray & Kelsie Saison
Every Nation Music
Go to www.everynationmusic.org for additional resources.

"Movements aren't sustained by preaching and writing alone but by the music and art that communicate the vision of the movement."
— Steve Murrell (President. Every Nation)

SONGWRITING

JOURNAL

SONG LIST

Title	Page

Title

Page

Song Title

Date   **Writers**

Key   **Bpm**

Theme

Toolbox

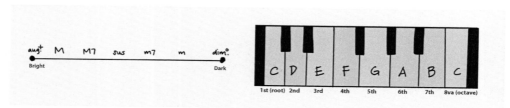

Song Title

Date   **Writers**

        Key   **Bpm**

Theme

Toolbox

Song Forms:	Literary Devices:	Rhyme Types:	
• ABABB	• Alliteration	• Perfect	• Couplet
• ABABCB	• Imagery	• Near/Slant	• Triplet
• ABCABC	• Personification	• Internal	• Enclosed
• AABAB	• Simile	• Alternate	• Ballad/Quatrain
• AAA	• Metaphor		
	• Anaphora		

Song Title

Date   **Writers**

Key   **Bpm**

Theme

Toolbox

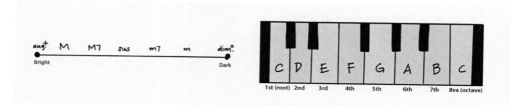

Song Title

Date   **Writers**

          Key   **Bpm**

    Theme

Toolbox

Song Forms:	Literary Devices:	Rhyme Types:	
• ABABB	• Alliteration	• Perfect	• Couplet
• ABABCB	• Imagery	• Near/Slant	• Triplet
• ABCABC	• Personification	• Internal	• Enclosed
• AABAB	• Simile	• Alternate	• Ballad/Quatrain
• AAA	• Metaphor		
	• Anaphora		

Song Title

Date   **Writers**

Key   **Bpm**

Theme

Toolbox

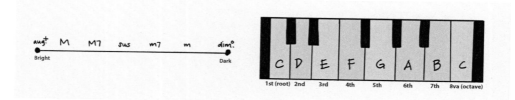

Song Title

Date   **Writers**

        Key   **Bpm**

Theme

Toolbox

Song Forms:	Literary Devices:	Rhyme Types:	
• ABABB	• Alliteration	• Perfect	• Couplet
• ABABCB	• Imagery	• Near/Slant	• Triplet
• ABCABC	• Personification	• Internal	• Enclosed
• AABAB	• Simile	• Alternate	• Ballad/Quatrain
• AAA	• Metaphor		
	• Anaphora		

Song Title

Date   **Writers**

Key   **Bpm**

Theme

Toolbox

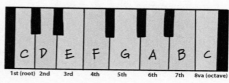

Song Title

    Date   **Writers**

        Key   **Bpm**

   Theme

Toolbox

Song Forms:	Literary Devices:	Rhyme Types:	
• ABABB	• Alliteration	• Perfect	• Couplet
• ABABCB	• Imagery	• Near/Slant	• Triplet
• ABCABC	• Personification	• Internal	• Enclosed
• AABAB	• Simile	• Alternate	• Ballad/Quatrain
• AAA	• Metaphor		
	• Anaphora		

Song Title

Date   **Writers**

Key   **Bpm**

Theme

Toolbox

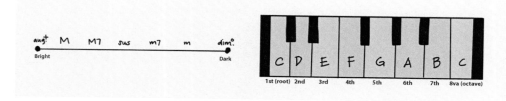

Song Title

Date   **Writers**

            Key   **Bpm**

Theme

Toolbox

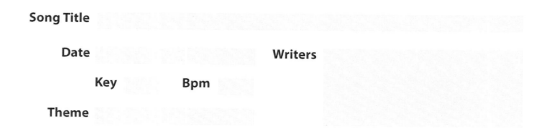

Song Title

Date　　　　　　　　　**Writers**

　　Key　　　**Bpm**

Theme

Toolbox

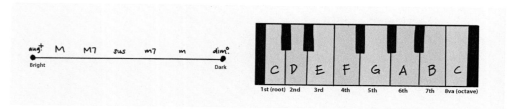

Song Title

Date   **Writers**

         Key   **Bpm**

Theme

Toolbox

Song Forms:	*Literary Devices:*	*Rhyme Types:*	
• ABABB	• Alliteration	• Perfect	• Couplet
• ABABCB	• Imagery	• Near/Slant	• Triplet
• ABCABC	• Personification	• Internal	• Enclosed
• AABAB	• Simile	• Alternate	• Ballad/Quatrain
• AAA	• Metaphor		
	• Anaphora		

Song Title

Date   **Writers**

Key   **Bpm**

Theme

Toolbox

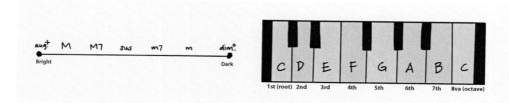

Song Title

    Date   **Writers**

        Key   **Bpm**

   Theme

Toolbox

Song Forms:	Literary Devices:	Rhyme Types:	
• ABABB	• Alliteration	• Perfect	• Couplet
• ABABCB	• Imagery	• Near/Slant	• Triplet
• ABCABC	• Personification	• Internal	• Enclosed
• AABAB	• Simile	• Alternate	• Ballad/Quatrain
• AAA	• Metaphor		
	• Anaphora		

Song Title

Date   **Writers**

Key   **Bpm**

Theme

Toolbox

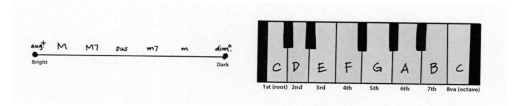

Song Title

Date   **Writers**

              Key   **Bpm**

Theme

Toolbox

Song Forms:	Literary Devices:	Rhyme Types:	
• ABABB	• Alliteration	• Perfect	• Couplet
• ABABCB	• Imagery	• Near/Slant	• Triplet
• ABCABC	• Personification	• Internal	• Enclosed
• AABAB	• Simile	• Alternate	• Ballad/Quatrain
• AAA	• Metaphor		
	• Anaphora		

Song Title

Date   **Writers**

Key   **Bpm**

Theme

Toolbox

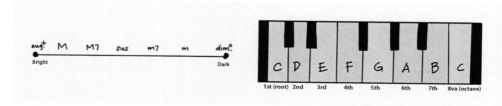

Song Title

Date   **Writers**

        Key   **Bpm**

Theme

Toolbox

Song Forms:	*Literary Devices:*	*Rhyme Types:*	
• ABABB	• Alliteration	• Perfect	• Couplet
• ABABCB	• Imagery	• Near/Slant	• Triplet
• ABCABC	• Personification	• Internal	• Enclosed
• AABAB	• Simile	• Alternate	• Ballad/Quatrain
• AAA	• Metaphor		
	• Anaphora		

Song Title

Date   **Writers**

Key   **Bpm**

Theme

Toolbox

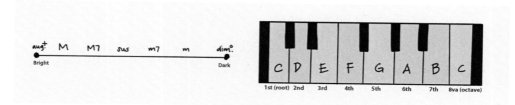

Song Title

Date   **Writers**

Key   **Bpm**

Theme

Toolbox

Song Forms:	*Literary Devices:*	*Rhyme Types:*	
• ABABB	• Alliteration	• Perfect	• Couplet
• ABABCB	• Imagery	• Near/Slant	• Triplet
• ABCABC	• Personification	• Internal	• Enclosed
• AABAB	• Simile	• Alternate	• Ballad/Quatrain
• AAA	• Metaphor		
	• Anaphora		

Song Title

Date　　　　　　　　　　**Writers**

Key　　　**Bpm**

Theme

Toolbox

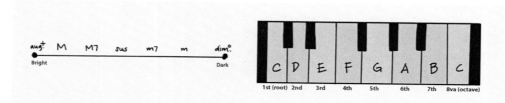

Song Title

    Date   **Writers**

          Key   **Bpm**

    Theme

Toolbox

Song Forms:	Literary Devices:	Rhyme Types:	
• ABABB	• Alliteration	• Perfect	• Couplet
• ABABCB	• Imagery	• Near/Slant	• Triplet
• ABCABC	• Personification	• Internal	• Enclosed
• AABAB	• Simile	• Alternate	• Ballad/Quatrain
• AAA	• Metaphor		
	• Anaphora		

Song Title

Date   **Writers**

Key   **Bpm**

Theme

Toolbox

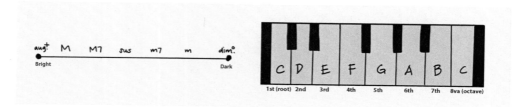

Song Title

Date   **Writers**

Key   **Bpm**

Theme

Toolbox

Song Forms:	Literary Devices:	Rhyme Types:	
• ABABB	• Alliteration	• Perfect	• Couplet
• ABABCB	• Imagery	• Near/Slant	• Triplet
• ABCABC	• Personification	• Internal	• Enclosed
• AABAB	• Simile	• Alternate	• Ballad/Quatrain
• AAA	• Metaphor		
	• Anaphora		

Song Title

Date   **Writers**

        Key   **Bpm**

Theme

Toolbox

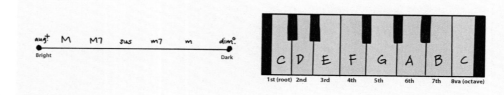

Song Title

Date   **Writers**

Key   **Bpm**

Theme

Toolbox

Song Forms:	Literary Devices:	Rhyme Types:	
• ABABB	• Alliteration	• Perfect	• Couplet
• ABABCB	• Imagery	• Near/Slant	• Triplet
• ABCABC	• Personification	• Internal	• Enclosed
• AABAB	• Simile	• Alternate	• Ballad/Quatrain
• AAA	• Metaphor		
	• Anaphora		

Song Title

Date   **Writers**

Key   **Bpm**

Theme

Toolbox

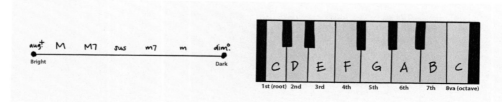

Song Title

    Date   **Writers**

        Key   **Bpm**

   Theme

Toolbox

Song Forms:	*Literary Devices:*	*Rhyme Types:*	
• ABABB	• Alliteration	• Perfect	• Couplet
• ABABCB	• Imagery	• Near/Slant	• Triplet
• ABCABC	• Personification	• Internal	• Enclosed
• AABAB	• Simile	• Alternate	• Ballad/Quatrain
• AAA	• Metaphor		
	• Anaphora		

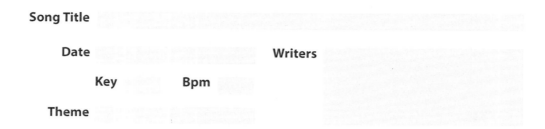

Song Title

Date   **Writers**

Key   **Bpm**

Theme

Toolbox

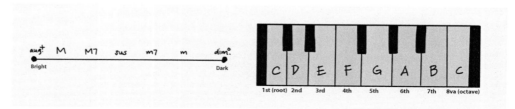

Song Title

Date   **Writers**

Key   **Bpm**

Theme

Toolbox

Song Forms:	**Literary Devices:**	**Rhyme Types:**	
• ABABB	• Alliteration	• Perfect	• Couplet
• ABABCB	• Imagery	• Near/Slant	• Triplet
• ABCABC	• Personification	• Internal	• Enclosed
• AABAB	• Simile	• Alternate	• Ballad/Quatrain
• AAA	• Metaphor		
	• Anaphora		

Song Title

Date   **Writers**

Key   **Bpm**

Theme

Toolbox

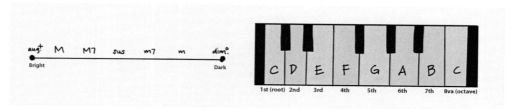

Song Title

    Date   **Writers**

        Key   **Bpm**

   Theme

Toolbox

Song Forms:	Literary Devices:	Rhyme Types:	
• ABABB	• Alliteration	• Perfect	• Couplet
• ABABCB	• Imagery	• Near/Slant	• Triplet
• ABCABC	• Personification	• Internal	• Enclosed
• AABAB	• Simile	• Alternate	• Ballad/Quatrain
• AAA	• Metaphor		
	• Anaphora		

Song Title

Date   **Writers**

Key   **Bpm**

Theme

Toolbox

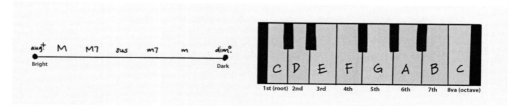

Song Title

Date   **Writers**

Key   **Bpm**

Theme

Toolbox

Song Forms:	*Literary Devices:*	*Rhyme Types:*	
• ABABB	• Alliteration	• Perfect	• Couplet
• ABABCB	• Imagery	• Near/Slant	• Triplet
• ABCABC	• Personification	• Internal	• Enclosed
• AABAB	• Simile	• Alternate	• Ballad/Quatrain
• AAA	• Metaphor		
	• Anaphora		

Song Title

Date　　　　　　　　　　**Writers**

Key　　　**Bpm**

Theme

Toolbox

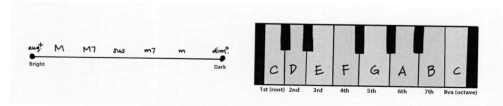

Song Title

Date   **Writers**

          Key   **Bpm**

     Theme

Toolbox

Song Forms:	*Literary Devices:*	*Rhyme Types:*	
• ABABB	• Alliteration	• Perfect	• Couplet
• ABABCB	• Imagery	• Near/Slant	• Triplet
• ABCABC	• Personification	• Internal	• Enclosed
• AABAB	• Simile	• Alternate	• Ballad/Quatrain
• AAA	• Metaphor		
	• Anaphora		

Song Title

Date　　　　　　　　　**Writers**

Key　　　　**Bpm**

Theme

Toolbox

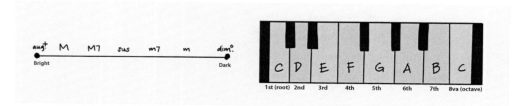

Song Title

Date   **Writers**

        Key   **Bpm**

Theme

Toolbox

Song Forms:	Literary Devices:	Rhyme Types:	
• ABABB	• Alliteration	• Perfect	• Couplet
• ABABCB	• Imagery	• Near/Slant	• Triplet
• ABCABC	• Personification	• Internal	• Enclosed
• AABAB	• Simile	• Alternate	• Ballad/Quatrain
• AAA	• Metaphor		
	• Anaphora		

Song Title

Date **Writers**

Key **Bpm**

Theme

Toolbox

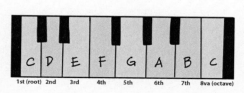

160

Song Title

    Date   **Writers**

          Key   **Bpm**

    Theme

Toolbox

Song Forms:	Literary Devices:	Rhyme Types:	
• ABABB	• Alliteration	• Perfect	• Couplet
• ABABCB	• Imagery	• Near/Slant	• Triplet
• ABCABC	• Personification	• Internal	• Enclosed
• AABAB	• Simile	• Alternate	• Ballad/Quatrain
• AAA	• Metaphor		
	• Anaphora		

Song Title

Date   **Writers**

Key   **Bpm**

Theme

Toolbox

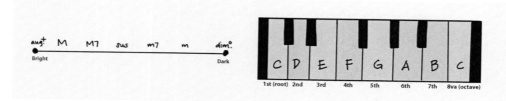

Song Title

Date   **Writers**

           Key   **Bpm**

      Theme

Toolbox

Song Forms:	Literary Devices:	Rhyme Types:	
• ABABB	• Alliteration	• Perfect	• Couplet
• ABABCB	• Imagery	• Near/Slant	• Triplet
• ABCABC	• Personification	• Internal	• Enclosed
• AABAB	• Simile	• Alternate	• Ballad/Quatrain
• AAA	• Metaphor		
	• Anaphora		

Song Title

Date   **Writers**

Key   **Bpm**

Theme

Toolbox

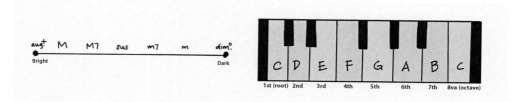

Song Title

Date   **Writers**

          Key   **Bpm**

Theme

Toolbox

Song Forms:	*Literary Devices:*	*Rhyme Types:*	
• ABABB	• Alliteration	• Perfect	• Couplet
• ABABCB	• Imagery	• Near/Slant	• Triplet
• ABCABC	• Personification	• Internal	• Enclosed
• AABAB	• Simile	• Alternate	• Ballad/Quatrain
• AAA	• Metaphor		
	• Anaphora		

Song Title

Date   **Writers**

         Key   **Bpm**

Theme

Toolbox

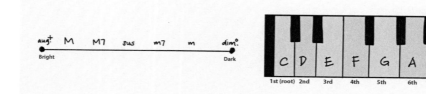

Song Title

Date   **Writers**

Key   **Bpm**

Theme

Toolbox

Song Forms:	***Literary Devices:***	***Rhyme Types:***	
• ABABB	• Alliteration	• Perfect	• Couplet
• ABABCB	• Imagery	• Near/Slant	• Triplet
• ABCABC	• Personification	• Internal	• Enclosed
• AABAB	• Simile	• Alternate	• Ballad/Quatrain
• AAA	• Metaphor		
	• Anaphora		

Song Title

Date   **Writers**

Key   **Bpm**

Theme

Toolbox

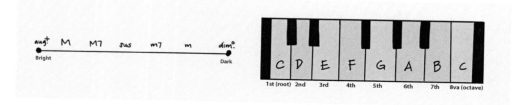

Song Title

Date   **Writers**

          Key   **Bpm**

     Theme

Toolbox

Song Forms:	**Literary Devices:**	**Rhyme Types:**	
• ABABB	• Alliteration	• Perfect	• Couplet
• ABABCB	• Imagery	• Near/Slant	• Triplet
• ABCABC	• Personification	• Internal	• Enclosed
• AABAB	• Simile	• Alternate	• Ballad/Quatrain
• AAA	• Metaphor		
	• Anaphora		

Song Title

Date   **Writers**

     Key   **Bpm**

Theme

Toolbox

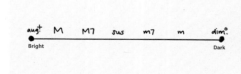

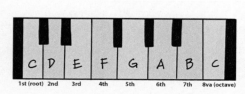

Song Title

Date   **Writers**

          Key   **Bpm**

Theme

Toolbox

Song Forms:	*Literary Devices:*	*Rhyme Types:*	
• ABABB	• Alliteration	• Perfect	• Couplet
• ABABCB	• Imagery	• Near/Slant	• Triplet
• ABCABC	• Personification	• Internal	• Enclosed
• AABAB	• Simile	• Alternate	• Ballad/Quatrain
• AAA	• Metaphor		
	• Anaphora		

Song Title

Date   **Writers**

Key   **Bpm**

Theme

Toolbox

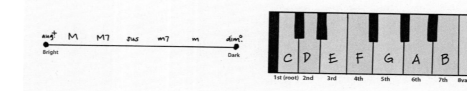